# Spirituals
## for Upper Voices

Edited by Rosephanye and William C. Powell

MUSIC DEPARTMENT

OXFORD
UNIVERSITY PRESS

# OXFORD
UNIVERSITY PRESS

Great Clarendon Street, Oxford OX2 6DP, England

Oxford University Press is a department of the University of Oxford.
It furthers the University's aim of excellence in research, scholarship,
and education by publishing worldwide

Oxford is a registered trade mark of Oxford University Press
in the UK and in certain other countries

ISBN 978-0-19-380519-4

Music and text origination by
Enigma Music Production Services, Amersham, Bucks.
Printed in Great Britain on acid-free paper by
Halstan & Co. Ltd, Amersham, Bucks.

# Preface

The African-American spiritual, considered by some anthropologists as the first true American folk song, was borne out of the enslavement of millions of Africans and African Americans between 1619 and 1865. Beginning on southern plantations, spirituals made their way to concert halls internationally, with their first appearance on the concert stage taking place in 1871 in a performance by the Fisk Jubilee Singers of Fisk University. The spiritual has since been exploited by composers and arrangers of every generation and in every classical music genre.

With its roots in slavery, the spiritual is of musical and historical importance to the heritage of its people. Music performed various functions in the slaves' lives, and was not distinguished as sacred or secular; it served a purpose for everyone according to their emotional needs and daily activities, including secret communication, work, entertainment, worship, and rebellion and protest. Hence, all African-American music can be ultimately traced back to the spiritual, which represents a significant body of vocal literature.

To ensure a performance that is respectful of its traditions, we recommend researching the spiritual as part of the preparation for performance. This could include information regarding the history and culture of the slave, and the function of music in slave society. Be sure to study the text to ascertain its meaning. Many spirituals have dual messages—one worshipful and apparent, and the other sociological and hidden or 'coded'. Some common examples are:

**Moses**    anyone who guided slaves to freedom in the North and Canada, such as the 'conductors' of the Underground Railroad, the Quakers, or individuals such as Harriet Tubman

**Jesus**    freedom, and anyone who guided slaves to freedom

**Jordan**    river, or the indication to follow or cross the river to make it to freedom

**Chariot**    any means of travel (carriage, wagon, group of escaping slaves) that led the way to freedom

**Sinner**    individuals such as the plantation owner, his wife, or the overseer, as well as slaves who betrayed the slave community or were undecided about escaping or revolting

**Heaven**    the northern United States, Canada, or any place to which slaves might escape to freedom.

An understanding of the historical backdrop and interpretative aspects of these songs is essential for a more meaningful performance for singers and audience alike.

Always work to convey the 'heart' of the spiritual, because emotional depth and expression are vital to the singing of this genre. Each arrangement in this collection as a different character. 'Scandalize my name', for example, is a rebuke of gossip in the slave community, intended to be performed with attitude and 'sassiness' (especially the spoken part at the end of the refrain). The arranger suggests that a roll of the neck or eye would be appropriate in performance. In contrast,

'Somebody's knockin' at yo' do'' is arranged with a sense of mystery, as the slave awaits the 'knock' that indicates the time at which escape to freedom will occur. 'Didn't my Lord deliver Daniel?' urges the escaping slave onward in the quest for freedom, while 'There is a balm in Gilead' expresses the depth of the slave's inner peace and hope while persevering in the midst of slavery.

The arrangements in this exciting collection vary in style, tempo, mood, and difficulty, allowing these wonderful songs to be appreciated by a wider audience. We are especially pleased to have had the opportunity to work with some of the most talented and respected arrangers of spirituals in the United States. We hope that you, as singers and conductors, enjoy the journey of experiencing and sharing the beautiful and powerful music that is the African-American spiritual!

# Performance Note

Aim to perform these songs with a classical vocal production; unless indicated, do not perform them in a gospel style, or with any other popular style of vocal production. (The spiritual and gospel genres are distinct, with gospel being a later African-American sacred music style that involves band accompaniment, hand-clapping, swaying, and a raw vocal production. Occasionally, spirituals are intentionally arranged in the gospel style, as in the case of 'In dat great gettin' up mornin''.) When performing spirituals, be careful not to swing rhythms unless indicated by the arranger, and do not substitute speed for rhythmic energy in the joyful songs such as 'This joy I have'. Finally, avoid using finger snaps with these songs, as historically these are regarded as disrespectful in the African-American church community.

To encourage a more authentic performance, the dialect pronunciation has often been included in the score. 'De' has been used in place of 'the', and similarly 'der', 'dis', and 'dat' instead of 'there', 'this', and 'that'. For 'de', the same rules of pronunciation should apply as in 'the': 'de' as 'dee' before a vowel ('dee earth') and 'da' before a consonant ('da glory'). Standard spellings have been intentionally retained in some cases, for example '*There* is a balm in Gilead', and these words should be pronounced as written. You will also notice variation across the collection in the spelling of some words, for example 'children', 'chillun', and 'chilrun'. This reflects the preferences of the arranger, as well as the different pronunciations used by the slaves, which varied according to location and cultural heritage. In order to achieve an authentic approach to singing with dialect, avoid over-enunciating the consonants.

To make the spirituals as accessible to as many choirs as possible, alternative notes have been added in some arrangements. Small notes are optional and can replace the main note if preferred—see, for example, the solo part in 'Lit'l David play on yo' harp', where a G may be sung instead of a B. Bracketed notes may be omitted entirely, such as at the end of 'I got a home in-a dat rock'.

Rosephanye and William C. Powell
March 2011

# Contents

# Arranger Biographies

**Rosephanye Powell** is a singer, arranger, and widely published composer. A graduate of the Florida State University, Westminster Choir College, and Alabama State University, she has distinguished herself as a researcher and interpreter of the African-American spiritual. She has served as a consultant for nationally syndicated radio, published articles on the subject, and presented lectures and performances at high schools, colleges, universities, music organizations, and churches around the United States. Her spiritual arrangements have been commissioned by nationally and internationally recognized professional choral groups and conductors. She was appointed Professor of Voice at Auburn University in 2001.

**William C. Powell** holds degrees from Alabama State University, Westminster Choir College, and the Florida State University. In 2001 he was appointed Associate Professor and Director of Choral Activities at Auburn University, where he conducts the chamber choir, concert choir, men's chorus, and gospel choir; he also teaches undergraduate and graduate courses in choral conducting, choral techniques, and choral arranging. In demand as a conductor, adjudicator, and choral music arranger, he has conducted All-State Choirs and at Carnegie Hall, Walt Disney World, and many choral festivals. He has lectured and presented at conference and workshop sessions for state, regional, national, and international meetings. His choral arrangements are published by Hal Leonard and Gentry Publications.

**Eurydice V. Osterman** has served as chair of the music departments at Northern Caribbean University in Jamaica and Oakwood University, Hunstville. A pianist, organist, and composer, she holds a Doctor of Musical Arts degree in composition and theory from the University of Alabama, and is the recipient of several awards for both composition and teaching. A member of several professional organizations, she has conducted workshops and seminars around the world and is a frequent guest lecturer.

**Byron J. Smith** was appointed Associate Professor of Music at Los Angeles Harbor College in 1999 and holds Bachelor and Master of Music degrees in Choral Conducting from California State University (Long Beach and Los Angeles). He is well known for his gospel compositions and arrangements, which are very popular in churches and schools worldwide, and he directs the world-renowned Spirit Chorale of Los Angeles, a professional ensemble specializing in the performance of spirituals and gospel music. He also enjoys success as a freelance producer and pianist, and has worked with many prominent artists in the jazz, R&B, gospel, and pop worlds. In 2008 he became First Vice President of the National Association of Negro Musicians, Inc.

**Mark Butler** is a composer, conductor, pianist, and music educator. He holds degrees in Music Education from Florida A&M University and the Florida State University, the latter concentrating on choral conducting. His compositions are quickly becoming favourites among the choral music world and are being performed at festivals, conventions, and venues throughout the United States. He has served as conductor and choral clinician at many workshops and festivals, including for the Association of American Schools of Central America in San Pedro Sula, Honduras and the Bahamas.

**Evelyn Simpson-Curenton** majored in music education and voice at Temple University and is highly respected as a versatile musician. As a performer, she has worked with numerous musical organizations, including Philadelphia's National Opera Ebony (now Opera North). Her compositions and arrangements have been programmed and commissioned by the National Symphony Orchestra, the Minnesota Orchestra, the late Duke Ellington, and opera singers George Shirley and the late Joy Simpson, her sister. Notably, Jessye Norman and Kathleen Battle have sung her arrangements at Carnegie Hall with the New York Metropolitan Opera Orchestra and Chorus, and on a Deutsche Grammophon CD, *Spirituals in Concert*. An associate of the Smithsonian Institution, she has lectured on early eighteenth-century black religious music and the music of African Americans during the Civil Rights era.

**Barbara W. Baker** is an internationally recognized conductor, educator, and arranger. She conducted the chamber, women's, men's, concert, and gospel choirs at Eleanor Roosevelt High School in Greenbelt, Maryland, for thirty years, with numerous successes at state, national, and international festivals. She has conducted honor choirs in the United States, Canada, Ireland, and Italy, and is a master choral clinician. A lecturer in African-American Gospel Music and Negro Spirituals, she has also contributed to several scholarly journals and textbooks. Her arrangements have been published by Boosey & Hawkes and she has a choral series with Alliance Music Publications. She holds degrees from the University of North Carolina at Greensboro; Teachers College, Columbia University; and the University of Maryland.

**Lela Anderson** is a Houston-based composer who received her Bachelor and Master of Arts degrees in Music Education from Prairie View A&M University, with further study undertaken at the University of North Texas and the University of Houston. Notable teachers include Robert Henry, David Cope, Michael Horvit, Karim Al-Zand, Paris Rutherford, Lucius Wyatt, and Toma Sita Lewis. Her music has enjoyed international success, with performances by school, church, university, and professional choirs, including the Choral Arts Society of Washington, the ACDA Central Region Honor Choir, and the National Baptist Convention Mass Choir.

**Damon H. Dandridge** holds a Bachelor of Music Education degree in choral music and voice from South Carolina State University and a Master of Music degree in choral conducting from the Florida State University. In 2010, following five years as Director of Choral Activities at Cheyney University of Pennsylvania, he began doctoral studies at Michigan State University, where he is also conductor of the Collegiate Chorale. He has been involved with the '105 Voices of History' initiative since its inception, serving as a National Conductor in 2008, and has worked with influential African-American composers and conductors such as Brazeal W. Dennard, Roland M. Carter, André J. Thomas, and the late Moses Hogan. His choral arrangements have been met with worldwide acclaim and have featured at numerous All-State and international festivals.

**David Morrow** is a native of Rochester, New York. He holds a Bachelor of Arts degree from Morehouse College, a Master of Music degree in choral conducting from the University of Michigan, and a Doctor of Musical Arts degree from the University of Cincinnati. He has been a member of the music faculty at Morehouse College since 1981 and directs the Morehouse College Glee Club. He is also Director of the Wendell P. Whalum Community Chorus, and Artistic Director and Conductor of the Atlanta Singers. In 2008 he was elected as President of the National Association of Negro Musicians, Inc.

**Jacqueline Hairston** is an ASCAP award-winning composer, arranger, pianist, and music educator, and a foremost expert on the spiritual and music from the African diaspora. Trained at The Juilliard School, Howard University, and Columbia University, she is a leading composer and arranger of spirituals. Her arrangements have been performed and recorded by internationally acclaimed singers such as Kathleen Battle, Grace Bumbry, and William Warfield, and orchestras including the London Philharmonic, the Lisbon Metropolitan, and the Oakland East Bay Symphony in California. Also interested in music and healing, she has released a piano CD entitled *Spiritual Roots & Classical Fruits: A Healing Harvest*.

**Robert L. Morris** is a conductor, composer, and choral clinician from Chicago. Holding degrees from DePaul University, Indiana University, and the University of Iowa, he has taught at Hampton University, Winston-Salem State University, Jackson State University, Macalester College, and Concordia University, Saint Paul. He has conducted at Carnegie Hall and other notable venues in the United States, Europe, and Australia, and his choirs have been lauded for their beauty of sound, expressiveness, and technical skill. His choral works appear in the catalogues of Alliance Music Publications, Walton Music, Shawnee Press, GIA Publications, Roger Dean Publishing Company, and Hidden Gems Music.

# Spirituals for Upper Voices

# Somebody's knockin' at yo' do'

Spiritual
arr. ROSEPHANYE POWELL (b. 1962)

Je - sus is knock- in' at yo' do'._____ Oh,\_\_\_\_ sin - ner,\_\_\_\_

do',_____ Je - sus is knock - in'. Oh,\_\_\_\_ sin - ner,\_\_\_\_

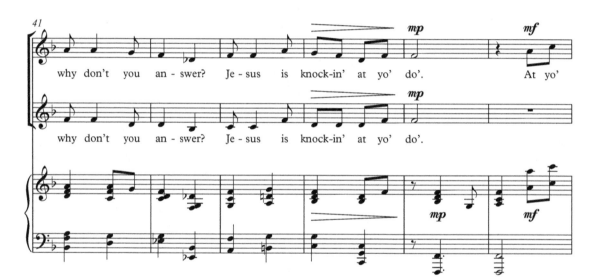

why don't you an - swer? Je - sus is knock-in' at yo' do'. At yo'

why don't you an - swer? Je - sus is knock-in' at yo' do'.

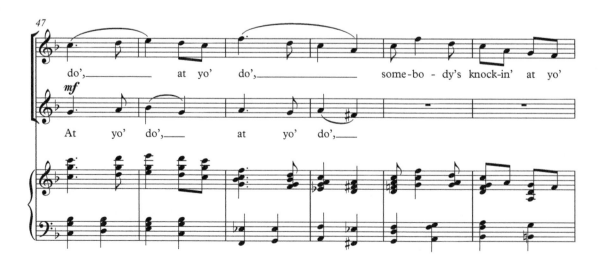

do',_____ at yo' do',_____ some-bo - dy's knock-in' at yo'

At yo' do',\_\_\_\_ at yo' do',\_\_\_\_

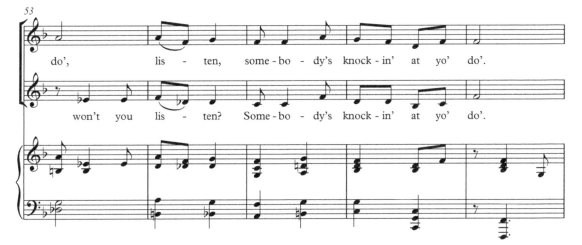

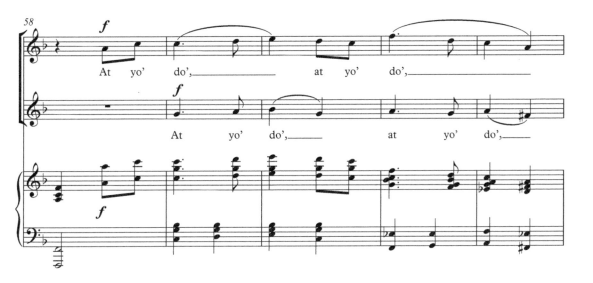

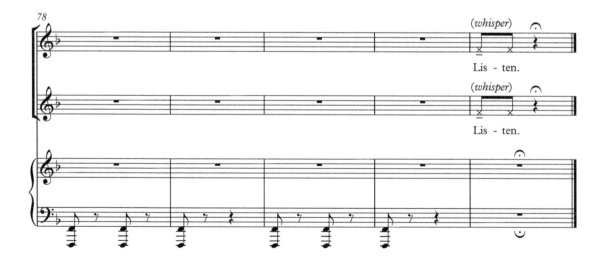

# Deep river

Spiritual
arr. WILLIAM C. POWELL (b. 1962)

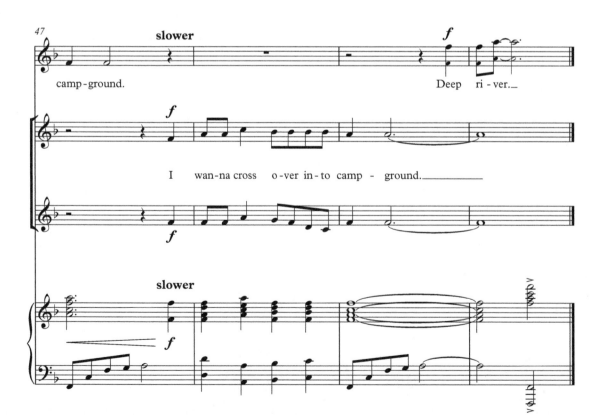

# I got a robe

Spiritual
arr. EURYDICE V. OSTERMAN (b. 1950)

you got - a shoes,    all    God's    chil-lun got - a    shoes.

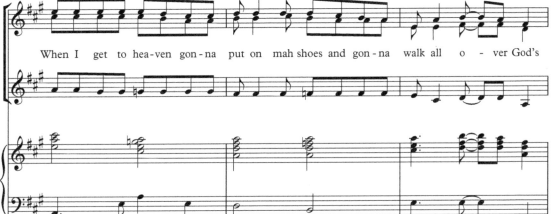

When I    get to hea-ven gon - na    put on    mah shoes and gon - na    walk all    o  - ver God's

hea - ven,_____    hea - ven,_____    gon - na    walk all    o  - ver God's

low,      sweet   cha  -  ri  -  ot,___      com-in'   for   to   car-ry   me

I   got    a crown,      you   got   a crown,      all    God's    chil-lun got a

home.             When I   get   to   hea-ven gon-na   put   on   mah crown and gon-na

crown.

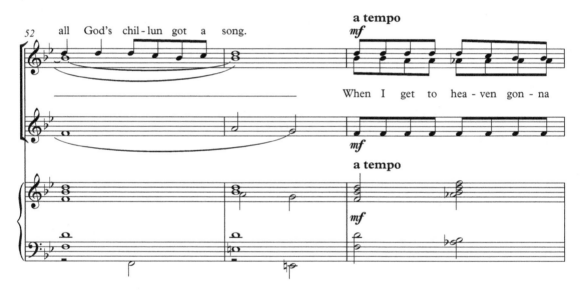

hea - ven,_____ hea - ven,_____ walk all o - ver God's

heav'n. Oh when de saints, oh when de saints, go march - in'

in, go march-in' in. I'm gon-na walk all o - ver God's hea-ven,_____

hea -ven.  I  got  a  robe  up  in - a  dat  king-dom,  I  got - a

shoes  up  in - a  dat  king-dom,  I  got  a  crown  up  in - a  dat  king-dom,  ain't  dat

good  news!_____  I'm  gon - na  walk  all  o - ver  God's  heav'n._____

# In dat great gettin' up mornin'

Spiritual
arr. BYRON J. SMITH (b. 1960)

*Each chorus may be performed twice, if desired.

great get-tin' up morn-in', fare thee well,___ fare thee well.___

Blow yo' trum-pet, Ga - briel.

Fare thee well,___ fare thee well._

Blow___

*dedicated to Dr Mary W. Roberts, Professor of Music (Emeritus), Florida A&M University, Tallahassee, FL*

# Let me fly

Spiritual
arr. MARK BUTLER (b. 1966)

*'de' should be pronounced as 'deh' (a short vowel without a diphthong).

Not so par-tic'-lar 'bout work-in' at de wheel,___ but I

jus' wan-na see how de cha-riot*___ feel. Now

let me fly, now let me fly,___ now let me fly to my home,___

*place the 't' sound on the staccato of beat 4

sing a-bout free-dom in ev - 'ry land,

pro-claim-in' hope for ev -'ry

man,

we'll

Join this jour-ney, make a stand,

we'll

we'll

*place the 's' sound on the staccato of beat 4

# Lit'l David play on yo' harp

Spiritual
arr. EVELYN SIMPSON-CURENTON (b. 1953)

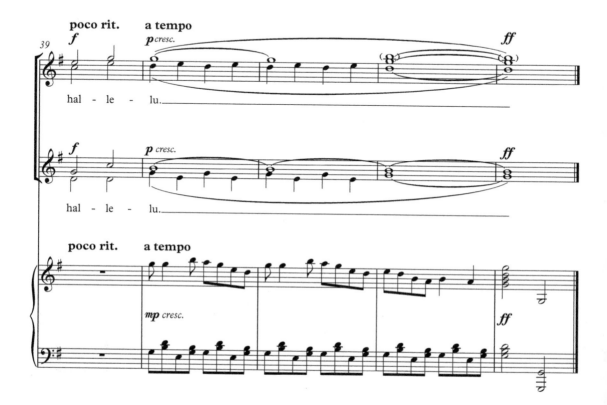

*in loving memory of Vincent Emeka Earl McCurty Alozie, grandson of Earl and Mary McCurty*

# There is a balm in Gilead

Spiritual
arr. BARBARA W. BAKER (b. 1945)

Choirs should stagger breathing throughout in order to achieve the required phrasing.

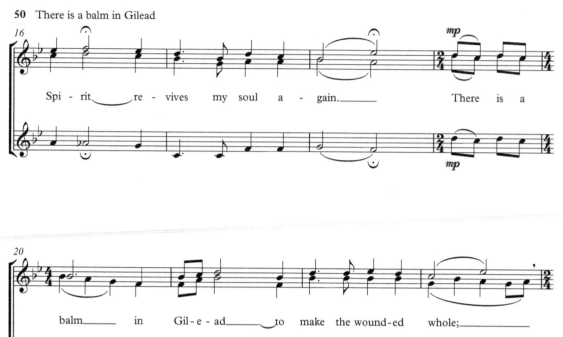

Spi - rit___ re - vives my soul a - gain.___ There is a

balm___ in Gil - e - ad___ to make the wound-ed whole;___

There is a balm___ in___ Gil - e - ad___ to heal the sin - sick

**rall.**          **a tempo**

If you can't preach like Pe - ter, *oo*___

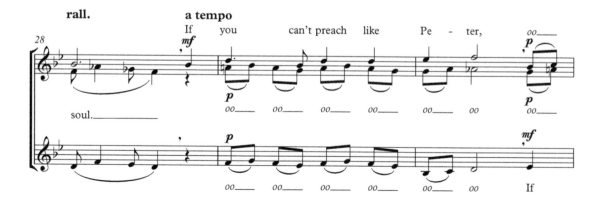

soul.___          *oo*___ *oo*___ *oo*___ *oo*___ *oo*___ *oo*          *oo*___

*oo*___ *oo*___ *oo*___ *oo*___ *oo*___ *oo*          If

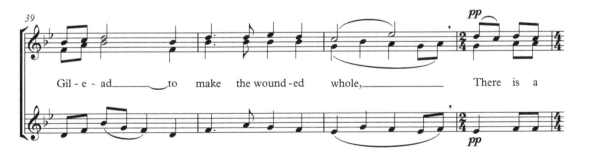

*to the glory of God and to my sister, Rita*

# I'm gonna sing

Spiritual
arr. LELA ANDERSON (b. 1950)

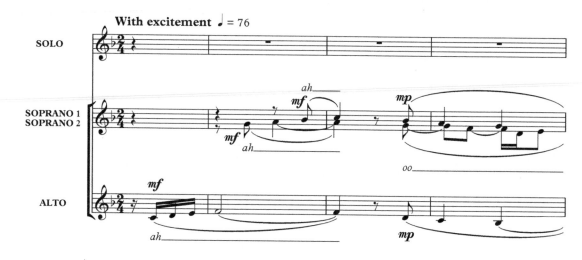

*'Mercy Lord, oh mercy Lord' should be performed by a single singer from within the choir, rather than the main soloist, who enters on 'Gonna pray'.

pray,                    pray— when the Spi-rit says  pray,      Just  pray,  just— pray, both

Oh my   Lord!          hm—          Yes,  my Lord, I'll   pray,—

night and day,        o  -  bey  the Spi-rit of the Lord.

o - bey—        my  Lord.   Shout  hal - le-lu-jah,

Gon - na

hal - le - lu - jah,        hal - le - lu - jah,        hal - le - lu - jah!

In the morn-in', in the eve-nin', I'll fol-low my Je-sus!

- bey,___ o - bey,___ o - bey,___ o - bey,___ o -

O - bey the Spi - rit of___ the Lord.___ Good God! I'll

- bey,___ o - bey.___ When I feel it mo - vin' I will o -

sing, pray, shout each day!_

- bey the Spi-rit, o - bey the Spi-rit, o - bey the Spi-rit, o - bey the Spi-rit, o -

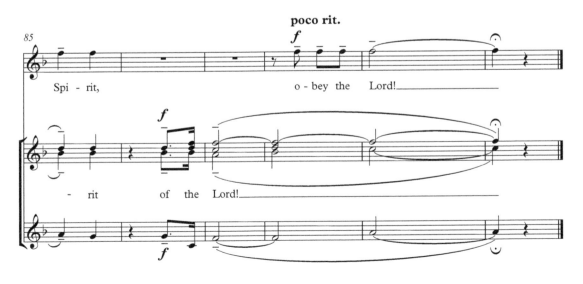

# Scandalize my name

Spiritual
arr. DAMON H. DANDRIDGE (b. 1977)

# Didn't my Lord deliver Daniel?

Spiritual
arr. DAVID MORROW (b. 1959)

whale, and the He-brew chil - dren from the fi' - ry fur - nace, then

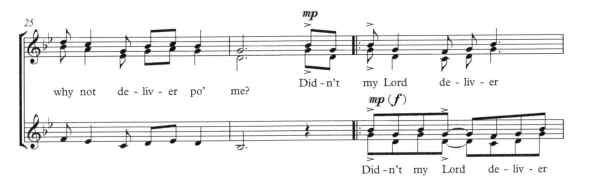

why not de - liv - er po' me? Did -n't my Lord de - liv - er

Did -n't my Lord de - liv - er

Dan - iel,__ de - liv - er Dan - iel,__ de - liv - er Dan - iel?__ Did -n't

Dan - iel,__ de - liv - er Dan - iel,__ de - liv - er Dan - iel,__ de - liv - er,

my Lord de-liv-er Dan - iel?__ Then why not de-liv-er po' me? Did -n't

did -n't my Lord de-liv-er Dan - iel,__ de-liv-er Dan - iel,__ de-liv-er me, po' me.__

ev-er-y star_____ will dis - ap - pear,_ yes, free-dom* shall_____ be,

be

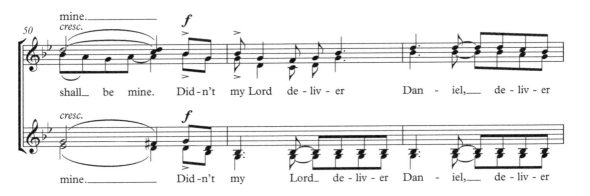

shall_ be mine. Did-n't my Lord de - liv - er Dan - iel,___ de - liv - er

mine._____ Did -n't my Lord_ de - liv - er Dan - iel,___ de - liv - er

Dan - iel,___ de - liv - er Dan - iel?___ Did -n't my Lord de - liv - er

Dan - iel,___ de - liv - er Dan - iel,___ de - liv - er, did -n't my Lord_ de - liv - er

Dan - iel?___ And he will de - liv - er, he will de - liv - er you!

*Alternative text: 'King Jesus' replaces 'yes, freedom'.

*in memory of my cousin, Jester Hairston*

# I got a home in-a dat rock

Spiritual
arr. JACQUELINE HAIRSTON (b. 1938)

* Sustain 'm'

# This joy I have

Spiritual
arr. ROBERT L. MORRIS (b. 1941)

*As an alternative, the 1st sopranos and altos may sing the small notes.